GuggenheimBILBAO

Art Spaces

An astonishing icon of the modern age, the Guggenheim Museum Bilbao opened its doors to the public in the autumn of 1997. Designed by the American architect Frank O. Gehry, the titanium-clad building is a milestone in the history of contemporary architecture.

It was born of the determination of the Basque Institutions to create a cultural centre of European importance and the desire of the Guggenheim Foundation to open museums in Europe in which to display its collections.

Variously described as a "metal flower" or a "benign sea monster", the museum is a feat of technical prowess and exceptional sculptural creativity. It has aroused an enthusiastic response world-wide and generated a dynamism that has propelled Bilbao into the post-industrial era.

Designed to accommodate all forms of modern and contemporary art, the Guggenheim Museum Bilbao is itself a masterpiece.

5,8
Code : 951 63
ISBN 2 86656 26

EDITIONS SCALA

9 782866 562632

GuggenheimBILBAO

Art Spaces

Francis Rambert

The history of the project

An astonishing icon of the modern age, the Guggenheim Museum Bilbao opened its doors to the public in the autumn of 1997. Designed by Frank O. Gehry, it is a milestone in the history of contemporary architecture, as significant in its time as the Centre Pompidou in Paris or the Sydney Opera House. Emblematic of urban renewal, the titanium-clad museum symbolises the regeneration of Bilbao. No modern building has ever aroused such international enthusiasm, nor received such massive media coverage, putting the Louvre pyramid in the shade. Its success has come as a surprise: who would have imagined that one day Bilbao, then the 56th-ranking European city, would welcome this flagship of culture?

Every architectural development has its own story. Gehry's Guggenheim was born of an unusual conjunction of political and cultural factors, the inspired outcome of an encounter between the public and private sectors. The determination of the Basque Administrations was a key factor in this prestigious undertaking. The fruit of cultural marketing and political enterprise, the museum has brought new dynamism to an ailing city. Just as Gaudi turned the spotlight on Barcelona, Frank O. Gehry has focused attention on Bilbao. With the Guggenheim, the city has entered the post-industrial era.

< The Guggenheim
  Museum Bilbao,
  at the heart of the city.

> Shipyards on the
banks of the Nervión.

It all began in the spring of 1991, when José Antonio Ardanza, President of the autonomous government of the Basque Country, invited Thomas Krens, director of the Solomon R. Guggenheim Foundation, to visit Bilbao. A major project was on the cards: the one to provide a home for the prestigious foundation in Europe – and why not in the Basque Country? At the time, Spain was gearing up for two other colossal building projects: the Universal Exhibition in Seville and the Olympic Games in Barcelona – the two major events of 1992. The challenge was to create "a cultural pole of European significance" at the heart of a declining industrial city. The Basques held to this course come wind or high water, with the result that an agreement between the Institutions and the Guggenheim Foundation was eventually signed on 13 December 1991.

Bilbao had been in economic decline since the 1970s. When its steelworks and shipyards were forced to close, this city of 1.3 million people suffered an unemployment rate approaching 30%. The terrible floods of 1983, when the River Nervión devastated the old part of town, had been the last straw, triggering an ambitious plan to revitalise Bilbao's urban fabric. A redevelopment scheme affecting the whole city was unveiled in 1989, and was soon extended to cover the entire metropolitan area, comprising thirty or so municipal districts. It involved demolishing and cleaning up the industrial sites along the "ría" (the river estuary), so as to free up areas of "flat" land in a predominantly hilly setting.

It was in view of this plan, the major investment envisaged and some of the projects already under way that the Guggenheim Foundation decided to install its new museum on Basque territory.

∧ The site before construction of the museum.

From heavy industry to the culture industry: what a transformation! As well as the vision of its elected government, Bilbao's regeneration must also be credited to the *Metropoli 30* association, which has invested in this major act of urban renewal alongside *Bilbao Ria 2000*, a company set up in 1992 as a joint venture involving the State (50%) and the various local authorities and public interests (Bilbao municipality 15%).

It was their idea to appeal to famous international names. Cesar Pelli, author of the world's highest twin towers in Kuala Lumpur, was asked to design a business centre in the middle of the planned 35-hectare city park, neighbouring the Guggenheim. And the British architect Norman Foster (designer of Hong Kong's new airport and the Berlin Reichstag) was invited to design Bilbao's new metro system, which came into service in 1995. The exceptional quality of his work in moulded concrete and steel, and the sophistication of his all-glass metro entrances, has been an important factor in changing the face of the city. They were immediately taken to heart by the locals and nicknamed "fosteritos".

Another part of the modernisation process was entrusted to Santiago Calatrava, one of Spain's greatest architect-engineers (author of Seville's grand viaduct and the Lyon Saint-Exupéry airport TGV station). He began the work of rehabilitating the River Nervión, constructing a magnificent glass-and-metal footbridge over its dark waters, just a few cable-lengths from the future Guggenheim. Following in the tradition of the Puente Colgante, the almost legendary transporter bridge built downstream of the city in 1893, Calatrava's footbridge, inaugurated in May 1997,

is emblematic of the new Bilbao. In the vicinity of the Guggenheim Museum, and also in direct contact with the river, is another new cultural facility, the Palace of Music. This building, designed by two young Spanish architects, Federico Soriano and Dolores Palacios, is easily recognised by its large bleached carcass, reminiscent of the city's former shipyards.

> The Bizkaia Bridge over
the Nervión estuary.

> The Zubi-zuri
pedestrian bridge,
by architect Santiago
Calatrava.

The Guggenheim Foundation from Frank Lloyd Wright to Frank O. Gehry

∧ Thomas Krens.

> The Solomon R. Guggenheim
Museum on Fifth Avenue,
New York.

The Guggenheim museum's implantation in the Basque Country was no random venture. It was part of an international strategy. Until that time, the Guggenheim's only other "export" was the Peggy Guggenheim Collection on the Grand Canal in Venice. Then, in the late 1980s, since only 7% of the museum's works were actually on display in New York, a decision was taken to circulate the collection, established in 1937. The way was open for further Guggenheim museums to open up in other parts of the world.

A number of cities, headed by Tokyo and Salzgue, put forward their claims. But it was the capital of the Basque Country which eventually won the day, fiercely determined to turn its back on industrial decline and make a fresh start in the field of culture and services.

The co-operative venture between Government and Foundation was based on a negotiated agreement: while the Basques offered their political backing and undertook to fund and manage the museum, the Americans contributed the Guggenheim collections and their long museological experience. The agreement stipulated that the Guggenheim Museum Bilbao would undertake to build up its own collection thereby adding to the Guggenheim Foundation's total artistic funds. So the Bilbao museum was to become one of the major cogs in dynamic cultural network of Guggenheim museums – a purpose attested to by its ambitious programme of temporary exhibitions.

While the Basque Administrations undertook to cover all the expenses incurred in setting up the museum, the Bilbao municipal authorities provided the site. Overall investment in the museum amounted to one billion francs, roughly a seventh of the sum invested in the highly controversial Bibliothèque nationale de France in Paris. In the context of a city severely affected by unemployment, even this might seem exorbitant, but it was the price to be paid for rehabilitating the image of the Basque Country. From this point on, the transformation of Bilbao was to prove irreversible.

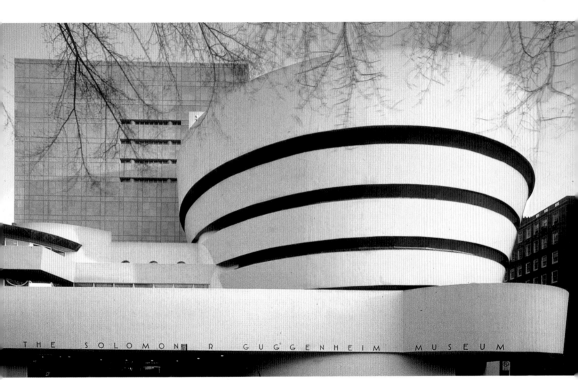

∧ Frank O. Gehry with
  J. Alberto Pradera,
  then Chief Executive
  Officer of the Provincial
  Council of Bizkaia.

For Thomas Krens, "a 21st-century museum must be able to house monumental 200-ton sculptures by Richard Serra as well as small drawings, and be equally hospitable to both". But the enterprising director of the Solomon R. Guggenheim Foundation, who had been looking to promote a suitable international development since 1988, was also aware that modern cultural developments are of necessity closely associated with the leisure industry. "We need to make art attractive, and architecture has an important role to play in this respect", he added, intent on turning his dream into a spectacular achievement.

The story goes that, in the spring of 1991, after a jogging session on the bridge which now pierces the museum, the Guggenheim director had a flash of inspiration: this was where the museum should be, on this industrial brown-field site on the left bank, but in touch with the Ensanche, the residential part of town. It should be there, not on any of the other sites proposed by the municipal authorities, which included a turn-of-the-century wine warehouse in the city centre awaiting conversion for some worthy purpose. It was at the heart of the "geocultural triangle" of Bilbao – as Thomas Krens called it – that the museum should be brought to birth.

The great challenge for Frank O. Gehry was to design a building that would bear comparison with the famous Guggenheim in New York, built on the edge of Central Park in 1959. It was no easy matter to follow in the footsteps of a giant such as Frank Lloyd Wright! At the dawning of the new century, Gehry was to amaze the world with an architectural gesture showing an incredible freedom of expression. In the Basque Country, the spiral effect of the New York museum underwent a dazzling acceleration. As a result, the Bilbao museum is a direct manifestation of the avant-garde spirit which has always been associated with the name of Guggenheim.

GUGGENHEIM MUSEUM BILBAO
SITE PLAN
FRANK O. GEHRY & ASSOCIATES, INC.

∧ Site plan drawn by
Frank O. Gehry, showing the
location of the museum.

> The museum, at the heart of a
rapidly growing city.

Like the Centre Pompidou in Paris, which revolutionised museum architecture in the 1970s, the Guggenheim Museum Bilbao sets out to celebrate modern and contemporary art at the dawn of the 21st century. But whereas Beaubourg is famed for its amazing flexibility, the Guggenheim Bilbao – which was designed to house works of all kinds and sizes – also has the quality of flamboyance. His design won Frank O. Gehry the 1998 Kiesler Prize, named after the visionary Viennese architect. The jury remarked on his "total courage and freedom of spirit".

The museum in the city

The museum stands right at the heart of Bilbao. Over and above the sense of movement imparted by its decidedly irrational geometry, the building's strength derives from the way it makes light of the constraints of the site. The architect had to make it straddle railway lines and allow for the passage of an existing motorway bridge. These features determine the Guggenheim's essentially urban character. By having the building rear up on the other side of the bridge like a monumental sculpture, Gehry has brilliantly combined the power of creation with the unique character of the site. The chaos of the industrial city is echoed by this expressionist building clad in futuristic titanium.

∧ One of the city's main traffic arteries, the Puente de La Salve was incorporated into the project.

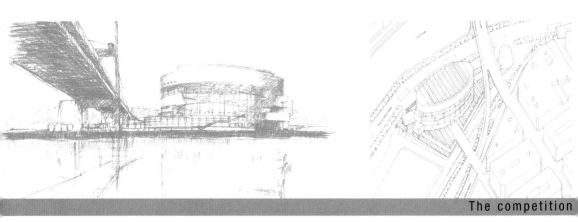

∧ The elliptical design proposed by the Japanese architect Arata Isozaki.

Frank O. Gehry was the winner of the international design competition held to choose the most suitable architect. In July 1991, his project for the building was selected, in Frankfurt, by a Basque jury which included Joseba Arregi, then Basque Minister of Culture, and Juan Ignacio Vidarte, the present director general of the Museum. Heinrick Klotz, former director of the Frankfurt Museum of Architecture, acted as referee in what was a very restricted consultation exercise.

Three stars of modern architecture had been invited to compete, each representing a different continent. So Bilbao became the focus of a confrontation between an Asian, two Europeans and an American, whose personalities and styles were bound to give rise to some highly individualistic solutions. It was a wide-open contest between the post-modern Arata Isozaki, a Japanese specialising in museums (including the SoHo Guggenheim in New York), the experimental Coop Himmelblau, a Viennese duo in the

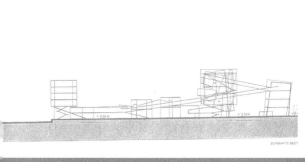

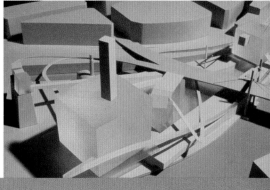

∧ The tripartite design
proposed by the Viennese
Coop Himmelblau team.

forefront of the avant-garde, and the unpredictable Californian Frank O. Gehry. The architects were given three weeks to produce a sketch and were told that they must integrate the La Salve viaduct into their projects, for as Thomas Krens put it: "the museum is wedded to the region by embracing the bridge".

But finally – between the elliptical museum proposed by the Japanese, the three cubes joined by a footbridge advocated by the Austrians, and the model of free architectural expression produced by the Los Angeles architect – the issue was never really in doubt. In contrast with its rather rigid rivals, Gehry's project exuded energy, conveying an impression of amazing dynamism. He was the only one really to make a feature of the bridge – a feat previously performed on the famous Museum Island in Berlin, which is traversed by an aerial metropolitan railway. Proof again that culture and infrastructure can co-exist in harmony.

Frank O. Gehry as architect

In the words of Frank O. Gehry: "Architecture should be attractive, accessible. It should encourage you to relax and open your mind". Gehry, who in 1989 was awarded the Pritzker Prize – regarded as the Nobel of architecture –, has remained one of the profession's greatest rebels, refusing to accept the dictatorship of straight lines and detesting anything that might embody perfection and deprive a building of emotion. On the contrary, he is the architect of the incomplete, having long advocated the idea that buildings are most beautiful when they are unfinished.

With the Guggenheim Museum Bilbao, Gehry seems to have provided proof to the contrary.

Gehry was born in Canada in 1929 and holds American citizenship. He began his career building houses on the Californian coast, including his own home, a modest building enlarged with plywood and galvanised wire mesh. At that time, only a few people knew of his work, the scale of which began to change when he designed a fanciful shopping centre and a car park for Santa Monica in the early 1980s. But it was his work in Europe that really brought him international attention. His design museum, a small-scale sculptural masterpiece, created in 1989 for the industrial firm of Vitra of Weil am Rhein (Germany), initiated a whole series of commissions. There followed the American Center at Bercy, Paris (1994), then a whimsical building, nicknamed "Ginger and Fred" by its owner, on the fringe of the old district of Prague (1996). When invited to design something for the Bilbao site, Gehry was still waiting for work to begin on the Disney auditorium in Los Angeles, which he had designed in 1987 and was thought "unbuildable" at the time.

< Frank O. Gehry, 1998.

Since the phenomenal success of the Guggenheim Museum Bilbao , Gehry has become the "star" of the architectural world and everyone is competing for his services. Current projects include the *Experience Music Project* in honour of Jimmy Hendrix in Seattle, a large auditorium for Chicago the Samsung museum in Seoul, and a winery for a Rioja vineyard in Spain. The Bilbao Guggenheim proved conclusively that Gehry has an acute sense of place and is able to bring life to a city

Original forms, spatial complexity, simple materials: these are the trade marks of Frank O. Gehry's work. In his own sober assessment: "My talent as an architect is perhaps simply that I am able to connect up all the moments of the project, from the rough sketch to the model to the finished building". Such a statement may well disappoint those who regard him as the incarnation of the architect-artist, for instance a Danish critic of architecture who sees him as "the only living architect to have completely succeeded in eliminating the boundary between architecture and the plastic arts".

Recognised as a great plastic artist, or even a sculptor, Gehry has always had easy relationships with fellow artists. He acknowledges that the concept of the Guggenheim Bilbao was the fruit of a discussion he had twenty years earlier with Daniel Buren – "mind you do not create a neutral box!", the French artist advised him – but it was Richard Serra who introduced him to the "magical" landscape of Bilbao.

Apart from the great New York sculptor – whose magnificent *Snake*, was specially commissioned by the Guggenheim Museum Bilbao – Gehry's favourite artists, or perhaps we should say accomplices, are Claes Oldenburg, whose works are featured in several of Gehry's buildings (an immense pair of binoculars for an advertising agency in Venice, California, some huge tools for the Vitra museum, etc.), Jasper Johns, Bob Rauschenberg and Al Bengston, for whom Gehry designed an attention-catching stage set in 1968 in Los Angeles, made from pieces of rough plywood and corrugated metal.

< *Torqued Ellipses* by Richard Serra.

∧ From left to right : Josu Bergara, the current Chief Executive Officer of the Provincial Council of Bizkaia, Richard Serra and Juan Ignacio Vidarte, Director General of the Guggenheim Museum Bilbao.

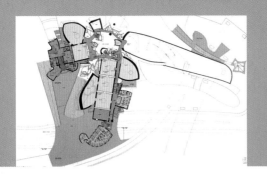

Seen – apparently emerging – from the waters of the Nervión, the museum could be taken for a benign sea monster. Although the metaphor of a "metal flower" is often quoted, the building undeniably belongs to a mysterious branch of the animal kingdom of which Frank Gehry is particularly fond: the great order of fishes.

For a long time the Californian architect had worked on organic themes and snakes and fishes were among his particular fetishes, though perhaps he had more of a penchant for fish than reptiles. Could it be because his grandmother kept trout in her bath-tub in Toronto? He maintains that: *"The fish is the symbol of movement. There is a whole series of buildings in which I have chopped off its head or its tail; the idea is to achieve abstraction, while keeping the quality of movement. "*

But the tendency towards sculpture in Gehry's projects for Kobe harbour in Japan or the Barcelona yachting marina found expression on a far greater scale in the Basque Country. Far more than a straightforward object, the museum turned out to be the city's integrating factor. While the sixty-metre tower with its V-shaped crown which rises on the far side of the Puente de La Salve is intended as a signal, the destructured body of the rest of the museum acts as an interface between two worlds.

Although the building has so many facets that it

is almost impossible to number them, we can distinguish two main "facades". On the city side, the museum, clad in ochre stone cut from a quarry at Huéscar, enters into dialogue with the old buildings of Bilbao, while on the river side the relationship it seeks to establish is quite different. Gehry has responded to the toughness of the city with strength, but with a total lack of aggression. All these shapes, however chaotic they may appear, convey a great sense of tenderness. It is a friendly, approachable building, as is evident from the vast esplanade laid out on the quayside, which leads to the large canopy and water garden.

∧ General view of
the museum from the
Deusto University.

^ The tower and the
promenade along the
river.

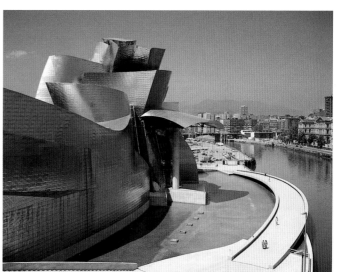

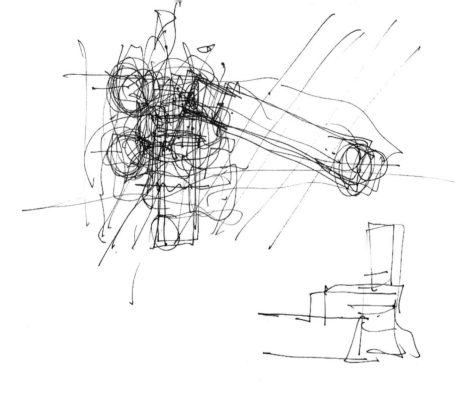

BILBAO   F. GEHRY

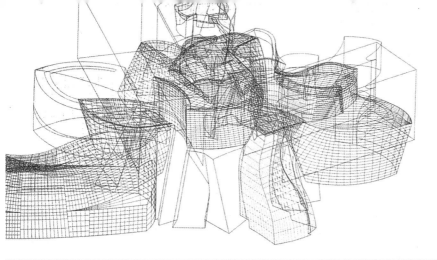

Project design and construction

It took four years to build the museum complex, which is arranged on three levels. It has a total surface area of 24 290 m², of which 11 000 m² is exhibition space. The work began in 1993 and represents a great technical feat. Like Spielberg, who brought long-dead dinosaurs to life by skilful modelling, Gehry used computer technology to model the Guggenheim Bilbao.

The complexity of the building and the integration of its different volumes were achieved using Catia modelling software developed by Dassault.
Thanks to this transfer of technology from the aerospace industry, we could say that the Guggenheim was designed in very much the same way as a Mirage jet fighter.

< First free-hand drawings.

∧ Computer-generated model.

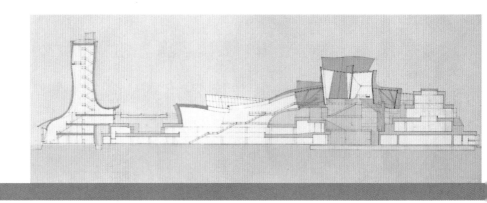

> Maquette of the
central Atrium.

Following double page:
First planned using
a wooden model, the
volumes and spaces were
then checked using Catia
software.

Gehry's team, working on a giant model, developed a completely new method, involving an almost unheard-of degree of precision. The use of the software to digitalise models to the nearest millimetre made errors of calculation virtually impossible, the computer being used to analyse surfaces and correct them in accordance with the structural and functional imperatives. The technology acted as a safety mechanism, while giving the architect the greatest possible creative freedom and unlimited scope for his imagination. The computer-assisted design techniques also had financial benefits, keeping waste to a minimum. The building is supported by an immense steel framework and it is reckoned that the computer, by guiding the milling machine used to cut up the huge steel beams with extreme precision, generated savings of 18%.

Before the Catia software was adopted, carefree imprecision was a hallmark of Gehry's practice, as the architect's philosophy was to suggest many possibilities rather than impose a single image. This is evidenced by the apparent muddle of his freehand drawings.

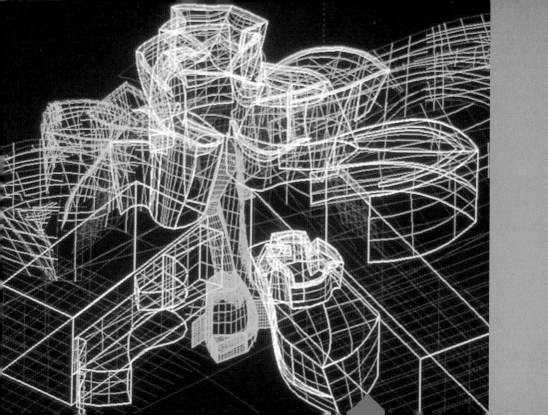

Of the Guggenheim Museum Bilbao's bold innovations, the one that most fascinates the general public is undoubtedly its titanium cladding, which is more an artist's material than a building material, so well does it react to the light. The museum's skin is a source of ever-changing reflections, whether under a blazing sun or the rain-charged clouds of the Basque Country.

The Bilbao museum, with its 32 000 m² of scales of pure, unalloyed titanium, broke new architectural ground in the use of this material. Renzo Piano had tried in vain to apply it to Kansai airport in Japan and, two years after the inaugu-ration of the Guggenheim Bilbao, the French architect Paul Andreu drew on Gehry's experience in using titanium as a cladding for the new Opera House in Beijing.

The advantage of titanium is that it can be applied in extremely thin sheets (just 0.40 mm thick), with each 61 x 120 cm panel overlaying 2 mm galvanised steel sheeting. At the same time, the irregular, hammered appearance of the material corresponds well to Frank O. Gehry's cherished idea of imperfection. The titanium used for the Guggenheim Bibao was specially laminated to accentuate the vibratory effect of the building.

< The city is always visible from the many windows set in the titanium wall.

∧ The museum, from the Puente de La Salve.

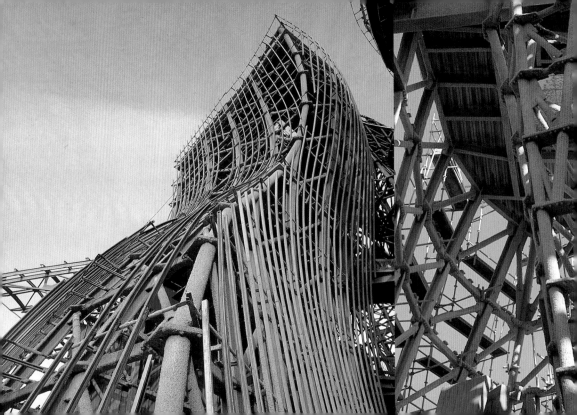

< Building work
in progress.

In the heart of the museum

The steps of what seems like an open-air amphitheatre lead the visitor down to the museum entrance, anticipating the breathtaking scene at the heart of the building. The 55-metre-high Atrium, inspired by the Expressionist vision of Fritz Lang's Metropolis, is architecturally the museum's most satisfying feature, using torsion effects to symbolise movement.
One is bound at this point to draw a comparison with Frank Lloyd Wright's magnificent rotunda for the Solomon R. Guggenheim Museum in New York, where the sense of movement derives from a spiral ramp, as both of these spaces form the heart of their respective buildings. The Bilbao Atrium, sculpted in stone and glass, regulates the flow of visitors to the museum's twenty galleries.

In fact, the museum itinerary comprises an amazing diversity of places and spaces. One of its great qualities is that visual contact with the city is never lost, thanks to breaches in the titanium between one generous-sized volume and the next. Light filters into every part of the museum through its flanks as well as through the roof areas.

The quality of a museum depends very much on the richness of its itinerary, and in this respect the Guggenheim Bilbao offers its visitors something very special. A good example is the complex of catwalks spanning the Atrium. They lead, for example, to the colourful room which for the inaugural exhibition was devoted to Sol LeWitt or, a stage further in this prodigious labyrinth, to the white room reserved at that time for Anselm Kiefer. Although some of the rooms have been criticised for their ordinariness, all criticism is silenced by the interplay of volumes whereby the height of some areas can be doubled to sixteen metres!

Another striking feature is gallery 104, an immense hall 130 metres long by 30 metres wide. This exceptional space was created more on the insistence of Thomas Krens than following the ideas of the architect himself. From a balcony, the visitor has a bird's eye view of this column-free gallery spanned at intervals by great white arches.

< The glass used in the museum is treated to protect the interior from heat and radiation.

Following double page:
The play of light inside the Atrium.
Exhibition galleries are organised around the central Atrium and connected by catwalks suspended from the roof.

∧ Jeff Koons's *Puppy* at
the museum entrance.

> The gala dinner held for
the grand opening, 1997.

Six months before its official inauguration by the King and Queen of Spain on 18 October 1997, the Guggenheim Museum Bilbao hosted a reception for an architectural elite, at which former holders of the Pritzker Prize gathered in the presence of Frank O. Gehry to honour the 1997 winner, Norwegian architect Svere Fehn.

The tables for the gala dinner were laid out in the museum's grand gallery, where Richard Serra had already installed his *Snake*, a sinuous piece 33 metres long and 4 metres high, weighing 170 tons, between whose angled plates of Cor-Ten steel the public were invited to make their way.

The Guggenheim celebrated its arrival on the international scene with a large inaugural exhibition, of which Jeff Koons *Puppy*, standing guard in front of the museum, was perhaps the most popular exhibit. This 12-metre-high dog was made of pots of flowers assembled on a metal framework.

What has become known as the "Bilbao effect", or more accurately the "Guggenheim effect" was felt from the very first day. Such was the

museum's success that even the most optimisti
forecasts – 450,000 visitors in the first year
were shattered by record attendances: by th
autumn of 1998, 1,360,000 people had visited th
museum, and in the first three years of its life th
attendance figures were 3.5 million. An analysi
of these figures confirms the institution's interna
tional appeal: 90% of these visitors were not from
the Basque Country. The Guggenheim Museur
Bilbao has become the second most popula

museum in Spain, behind the Prado in Madrid. Nor do these figures take into account the evening events organised every three days in the Atrium. At the same time, thanks partly to the attraction of Gehry's Guggenheim, attendance figures for the city's fine arts museum have doubled (over 200,000 visitors in the year 2000). So Bilbao has become the first link in a transatlantic chain. Barely two months after the inauguration of the Basque museum, the Guggenheim Foundation opened a branch in Berlin, capital of a reunited Germany. "Our ambition – declared Juan Ignacio Vidarte, director general of the Guggenheim Museum Bilbao, announcing that the institution had already enrolled 10,000 "friends" – is to create one of the world's foremost crossroads and exhibition centres for modern and contemporary art".

< Official reception in the Atrium, 1997

∧ Gala dinner for the opening of the exhibition *China: 5,000 Years*, 1998.

The first exhibitions

> The exhibition *The Art of the Motorcycle*, staged by Frank O. Gehry, 1999-2000.

Following double page: Richard Serra's *Snake* housed in the long gallery (130 metres long by 30 metres wide). *Shadow and Mouth*, Juan Muñoz.

Will the Guggenheim Bilbao one day exhibit *Guernica*? It is impossible to say, but Frank Gehry did design a special room to house Picasso's famous painting, in a gallery in the upper part of the Atrium. When the museum first opened, this area was occupied by Claes Oldenburg's giant *Soft Shuttlecock* with its huge drooping feathers during the opening exhibition "The Guggenheim Museum and the Art of this Century".

This inaugural exhibition presented a wide-ranging panorama of modern art (figurative, abstract, primitive, cubist, neo-expressionist, post-minimalist, pop, conceptual), bringing together over 350 works by artists as diverse as Kandinsky, Chagall, De Kooning, Rothko, Braque, Basquiat, Buren, Rauschenberg, Boltanski and Motherwell. The major Spanish and Basque artists, such as Antoni Tapiès and Eduardo Chillida, were also well represented. The museum was clearly ushering in a new generation of cultural facilities in which artists were only too happy to exhibit their work. This was largely due to the quality of the exhibition areas designed by Frank O. Gehry. Firstly, though totally immersed in the world of art, the visitor never loses contact with the city, of which there are frequent tantalising glimpses. Then his itinerary is marked at intervals by

fascinating installations: the columns designed by the American Jenny Holzer on which LEDs spell out texts in English, Spanish and Basque; or the series of seventeen panels of different sizes painted by the high priest of the Italian trans-avantgarde movement, Francesco Clemente, some of which serve as magnificent door frames to adjacent rooms.

As he progresses through rooms and over cat-walks, the visitor is eventually led to the grand gallery featuring Serra's *Snake*, one of the exhibits which is really at one with the architecture, and here the special creative relationship between Gehry and Serra takes on a new dimension. During the inaugural exhibition, visitors could stroll around works by Robert Morris and Lawrence Weiner, or the giant Swiss army knife with open blades by Claes Oldenburg. As well as site-specific commissions from various artists, the Guggenheim Bilbao began with a collection of a hundred or so works. Its first acquisitions were examples of Abstract Expressionism, by artists such as Mark Rothko, Willem De Kooning and Clyfford Still. Their works form the basis of the collection, together with works by contemporary artists such as Yves Klein, Sigmar Polke and Anselm Kiefer.

The contemporary Basque and Spanish art is also represented by Cristina Iglesias, Txomin Badiola, Prudencio Irazabal, Juan Luis Moraza and Miquel Barceló.

< Mural painting by Sol LeWitt in gallery 208 at the opening exhibition.

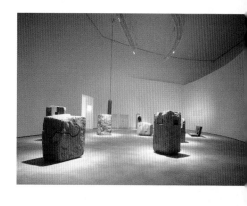

Since the inauguration, there has been a whole series of exhibitions, focusing on both past ("China : 5 000 years", "From Degas to Picasso") and present (*The Tower Wounded by Lightning*, Clemente). One of the most striking was Richard Serra's exhibition of *Torqued Ellipses*, a selection of which had previously been exhibited in the hangar of the Dia Center in New York. In the spacious setting of the Bilbao museum's gallery 104, the San Francisco sculptor sought to offer sensations different from those instilled by the *Snake* experience. These contorted forms had a special connection with Bilbao, influenced by

Gehry's example, Serra had discovered how much a sculptor could benefit from using the Catia software. The sail-like plates of Cor-Ten had been designed using computer technology, as had the Guggenheim itself.

The year 2000 has seen exhibitions as varied as "Amazons of the Avant-Garde"; "Changing Perceptions: The Panza Collection at the Guggenheim Museum". But special mention must be made of Frank O. Gehry's "The Art of the Motorcycle", for which the museum's architect assumed the role of stage designer. The exhibition featured a hundred or so models dating from

< *Levitas*, Javier Pérez.

^ Exhibition devoted to Eduardo Chillida, 1999.

1868 to 1999, including an Agusta from the collection of King Juan Carlos, displayed on a black undulating surface. As far as the permanent collections are concerned, important events have been the presentation of *Too Late for Goya*, an installation by Francesc Torres, and some major retrospectives featuring, for instance, Richard Long, the great protagonist of Land Art, and the German neo-expressionist Anselm Kiefer. Photography has also been prominent, with portraits by Sugimoto (previously unshown examples from his dioramas series), and the "Contemporary Photography: An Expanded View" exhibition – all in all, a series of events which confirms the Guggenheim Museum Bilbao's international vocation as a place of choice for the avant-garde.

< *Installation for Bilbao* by Jenny Holzer.

< *Three red Spanish Venuses*, Jim Dine.

> *F.O.G.*, Fujiko Nakaya,
> 1998.

The construction of the Guggenheim has been paralleled by an economic phenomenon thanks to the economic activity generated by the museum. Of course, this has to be set in the general context of the overall economic renaissance of Bilbao, but a survey carried out at the end of the year 2000 reckons the spin-off from the museum to have been approximately 500 million dollars, five times its initial cost – an incredible return on the investment it represents. The cruise ships now put in at Bilbao to enable their passengers to visit the museum.

If there is a lesson to be learned from the story of the Guggenheim Museum Bilbao, it is that culture seems to make itself at home in run-down industrial areas. This would seem to be confirmed by the experience of London's Tate Modern, installed in the year 2000 in a disused power station. But the Guggenheim Museum Bilbao will remain the shining example of this kind of urban regeneration, for the world as a whole and for the Basque Country, which continues to pursue its policy of cultural openness. Since the inauguration of

Frank O. Gehry's masterpiece, another splendid facility has appeared on the scene: the Kursaal built on the seafront in San Sebastian by Rafael Moneo, another Pritzker Prize winner.

Current projects, such as the new deep-water harbour and the extension of Foster's metro to improve communications in the metropolitan area, will be joined in the coming years by Bilbao's grandest project of all: the development of a five-kilometre strip of land between the heart of the city and the mouth of the river. A whole process of transformation is under way.

As the construction of the new harbour begins to free up sites on the riverbanks, the railway lines running parallel with the river will be channelled underground to make way for a large area of parkland – a welcome transformation of the area at the foot of Bilbao's green hills.

Museo Guggenheim Bilbao,
Abandoibarra 2,
48001 Bilbao
(nearest metro Moyua)
Tel. 00 (34) 94 435 90 80
http://www.guggenheim-bilbao.es

Information

Opening times
Tuesday to Sunday from 10 a.m. to 8 p.m.
Closed on Mondays.
In July and August, the museum is open every day, from 9 a.m. to 9 p.m.

Entry charges
Charges vary from exhibition to exhibition. Admittance is free for children under 12. Tickets are valid for the whole day and it is possible to leave the museum and return later.
Tickets can be purchased in advance by telephoning 00 (34) 94 435 90 80 (Tuesday to Sunday, 10 a.m. to 8 p.m.).

Guided tours
The Guggenheim Museum Bilbao organises free guided tours of the building, temporary exhibitions and the permanent collection. Audio-guides are available to visitors. For a private guided tour, please call 00 (34) 94 435 90 80 (Tuesday to Sunday, 10 a.m. to 8 p.m.).

Other services
The museum has a 350-seater auditorium, a bookshop and a café/restaurant with terrace overlooking the Nervión.

A few figures :

Total site area
32 700 m$_2$

Museum area
24 290 m$_2$

Total exhibition area
(20 galleries)
11 000 m$_2$

Photographic acknowledgements

FMGB Guggenheim Museum Bilbao: p. 6, 7, 12, 13, 14, 16, 17, 24, 37, 38.
FMGB Guggenheim Museum Bilbao, Erika Barahona Ede: p. 2, 3, 10, 15, 20, 22, 23, 25, 26, 27, 34, 35, 37, 40, 42, 43, 44, 45, 46, 47, 49, 50, 51, 52, 54, 55, 56, 57, 58, 59, 60, 62, 64.
Frank O.Gehry & Associates: pp. 28, 29, 30, 31, 32, 33.
David Heald: p. 11.
Coop Himmelblau: p 19 (left).
David Hornback: pp. 5, 8, 9.
Arata Isozaki: p. 18.
Markus Pillhofer: p 19 (right).
Aitor Ortiz: pp. 36, 38, 39.

Translation
Simon Knight
Graphic design
delepière**damour**
Photoengraving
Bussière
Printing
Editoriale Lloyd, Trieste
Copyright registered: July 2001

GuggenheimBILBAO

English